W9-CKT-440

011.6 CE32a

ENTERED FEB 2 0 2003

THE AFTERLIFE OF OBJECTS

PHOENIX POETS

COLUMBIA COLLEGE LIBRAR
600 S. MICHIGAN AVENUE
CHICAGO, IL 60605

The
Afterlife
of
Objects

DAN CHIASSON

THE UNIVERSITY OF CHICAGO PRESS
Chicago and London

DAN CHIASSON is assistant professor of English and direc-
tor of the poetry center at the State University of New York at
Stony Brook. His poems have appeared in magazines such as
*Paris Review, Ploughshares, Slate, Threepenny Review, Partisian
Review,* and the *New Yorker,* where he was featured as a 2001
"Debut Poet."

The University of Chicago Press, Chicago 60637
The University of Chicago Press, Ltd., London
© 2002 by The University of Chicago
All rights reserved. Published 2002
Printed in the United States of America

11 10 09 08 07 06 05 04 03 02   1 2 3 4 5

ISBN: 0-226-10377-3 (cloth)
ISBN: 0-226-10378-1 (paper)

Library of Congress Cataloging-in-Publication Data

Chiasson, Dan.
    The afterlife of objects: poems / Dan Chiasson.
        p.   cm.—(Phoenix poets)
    ISBN 0-226-10377-3 (alk. paper)
    ISBN 0-226-10378-1 (pbk.: alk. paper)
    I. Title   II. Series
    PS3603.H54 A68 2002
    811'.6—dc21

                                    2002002852

  ♾ The paper used in this publication meets the minimum
requirements of the American National Standard for
Information Sciences—Permanence of Paper for Printed
Library Materials, ANSI Z39.48–1992.

For Annie Adams

811.6 C532a

Chiasson, Dan.

The afterlife of objects

In reflecting on the *modus operandi* of our consciousness of time, we are at first tempted to suppose it the easiest thing in the world to understand. Our inner states succeed each other. They know themselves as they are; then of course, we say, they must know their own succession. But this philosophy is too crude: for between the mind's own changes *being* successive and *knowing their own succession,* lies as broad a chasm as between the object and subject of any case of cognition in the world. *A succession of feelings, in and of itself, is not a feeling of succession. And since, to our succession of feelings, a feeling of their succession is added, that must be treated as an additional fact requiring its own special elucidation.*

— WILLIAM JAMES, *Principles of Psychology*

We cannot fall out of this world.

— CHRISTIAN DIETRICH GRABBE, *Hannibal*

Contents

III

IV

Acknowledgments

Grateful acknowledgment is made to the following publications in which these poems, sometimes in different versions, first appeared:

Agni: "Stealing from Your Mother," "Vermont"
The New Yorker: "The Anatomy of Melancholy," "Nocturne," "Self"
Paris Review: "Dream of the End of Reading"
Partisan Review: "Peach Tree," "Visit"
Ploughshares: (guest editor, Jorie Graham) "Anonymous Bust of a Man,"
          "Orange Tree"
Slate: "Leverett Circle," "Poem," "The Sensible Present Has Duration"
Threepenny Review: "Boston"
The Western Humanities Review: "Cicada"

"Spade," "Purple Blouse," and "After Ovid" appeared as sections of *Ovid at Tomi* in the book *My Favorite Plant: Writers and Gardeners on the Plants They Love* (Farrar, Straus, and Giroux, 1998).

*

Thanks to everyone who read these poems in drafts, especially my teachers. Special gratitude to my mother, Linda Chiasson.

I

Nocturne

Do our words count so late at night,
this late do even these words count?

In life I was heroic at times, at
other times quiet as a mug of milk.

I saved a man I swear, but afterward
wherever I walked I saw one drown.

Men cry their names out when they die
and one man as he died cried *Dan*.

Back then I thought the water was air;
I thought the body was a bar of soap.

Other and Other made a ladder and up
to the top I climbed and saw America.

Other and Other made a mirror and in
I stepped and watched the water heal.

Of course there was no *man* no *Dan,*
I'm speaking in terms of the moon—

and anyway this late at night our words
can't count. Not even these words count.

Your Stone

Here's your stone he said *what for* I said *for your girl* he said
and left me alone in the bedroom strewn with punctured cans.

They bring the fire so close to their face I thought every time
the living room flashed and wild cries climbed to ecstatic silence.

Ecstatic silence: just yesterday alone in my study I heard
the neighbor's child practicing scales on a rented clarinet

just last night when your crying ended and you fell asleep
I prayed to be made inanimate, a hand-me-down mattress.

But tonight the little crystal called forgetfulness, the postures
of delight and appetite, and the beautiful girl said *what's your name?*

Vermont

I was the west
once. I was paradise.

My beauty ruined me: the old
excuse. Perhaps

if I was rich, remote
or fine—but paradise

is always just
too close, too coarse.

Men made me;
though in memory they seem
more steel than

flesh, more copper
than intelligence or whim, ambition, will—

what makes men, anyway? Always
groaning on the far end

of some lever, sharpening some blade.

If I were farther, Jupiter
or Babylon, the ocean
bottom, I

might have been a story. Stories never ruined anybody.

But paradise is always only
close enough, just

west, the next, the next, the sun
halved every evening on the same line of

the poem, the poem itself

a minute in the history of minutes. Then
decorative and north,
unstoried, white. And after that, pure

thoroughfare. My signs are written twice.

"*The Sensible Present Has Duration*"

O blistering cabinet

*

O mahogany, O birch pipes,
pipe rack, hardcover

books—*The Last Convertible, Trinity,*
The Royal Wedding,

biography of Patton.
Railroad spike inscribed

On your thirtieth year as
a soldier, from the 73rd.

Mail-order crest, name etched
in "runic" script.

O photograph

*

swollen
by false cures, my uncle

age nine, no more
appointments, strawberry-sized

tumors dotting his spine,
O icicle, formed for dissolution,

"pride" or portent. Military olive.
Toque, wool surrogate.

He stands beside a sapling
lilac, white twin, blossoming.

O window

*

Outside, my grandfather wheeling
a pesticide tank

from tree to tree, spraying everything
with thick, white foam—

bark, leaf, apple flesh—
salting the garden

with handfuls of red sand, dissolving
aphid, Japanese beetle, horned tomato worm

as thick as rope. Gone
in an instant, emerging

from his fiberglass outbuilding shed, helving
an axe, bright blade, pine handle,

to eliminate
a dwarf peach weakened by nesting beetles.

O ordinary axe

*

lilac, uncle, window, cabinet
lost, not lost, mere home

I merely left, look away
made elegy: a book's

fifth edition, its
yellow cover, not the available red,

instruction manual
for an old-world

Beta VCR, *The Way*
split by a nylon dividing ribbon.

*

An out-of-print book.

A remainder.

Boston

When it was time to pass outside myself I sought
the nearest
famous city, nearest

place whose boundaries were not contiguous with mine—

downstate, wax autumn sprayed
with the dust of the pulverized hillside, miles

of it dynamited and all
I-89 made
rabbit warren and collapsing domino.

Inside
the famous city, no one knew me, everyone

walked carrying books
called *Tintoretto, Giotto*—

frescoes set
by the blaring of an

ambulance, a man miming

his mother's lullabies, a lady
purring *Rattlesnake O Rattlesnake*

to calm her spastic arm. Ahead,

the "horrific glazed
perpendiculars of the future"—

and once I saw a man trying
to steady an
aquarium on his bent knee, nearly

impossible to carry,
lose his

grip and fish and glass were everywhere.

"The Anatomy of Melancholy"

for D. T.

I

You turned the lights out to read "Lycidas," holding the very berries
"harsh and crude" Milton held reluctantly for his school friend.

Then memory, imprecise but more precise than mine, went rummaging
for ivy and laurel, laurel and myrtle, all the tangled syntax candor

still takes to be revealed, even between two friends. Later, you dreamed
the whole poem came unspooled and lay tangled around your feet.

II

Or is Burton's *Anatomy* your model, making sadness
excess and excess precision, piles of the stuff:

Burton, who blackened his forearms with melancholy ink?
One time we tried crushing our Zoloft up and doing lines
of it, but you were right, or Burton was: it "misaffected" us
and made us "bursten-bellied, writhren and blear-eyed."

III

Your dissertation pictured seventeenth-century men picturing grief,
that ocean bottom dark but for occasional punk-rock

coral and ghoulish man-o-wars that hover over it.
You followed Milton following his school friend down

the monstrous deep to find a likeness of your own sad mind,
a coral ruler with a coral scepter sitting on a coral throne.

Paul 1:13

When I became a man my childish things
began to pile up
and putrefy. They were like heirlooms, other people's

things trying to mean *my past*
inside the gilt
upholstered future they arranged for me.

I feared them years before the forklift
came and dumped
them in the living room.

Now it is night, and all I am
is souvenirs of youth:
toy hammer, donkey's ass, and cancer ward.

Dactyls after Driving through Nevada

for J. P.

If at a party a stranger approaches,
       friend of a friend or cousin from home
O how will I greet him? Crisscrossing

       Nevada, highwayside shrines
write *wreck* in italics: one
       pilgrimage done, another begun.

What was it you said about
       guardrails, their miles and
miles of comical silence? Or road signs,

       so weird in the ultimate landscape—
the nothingness named; or what
       seems to be nothingness, canyon and

trace, evergreen grove, the rivers with
       Spanish and Indian names—
and what if that friend of a friend had a

brother returning from Europe now
ten years ago, a brother half
        hero, half slacker, merely desires and

lovely pretensions (the *Gauloises*
        and Sartre in his carry-on
bag) turned into myth over

        Lockerbie, Scotland, spasm and
flash, suddenly any boy falling alone
        through the sky, found in a creamery?

Io

Why must my father's love be written in gibberish hieroglyphs
thought a Hawaiian girl named for one of Jupiter's moons

so she moved to Boston to be near the other ocean, the one
that knew not a thing about the unthinkable act or the regime

of compulsory tenderness that followed anon and when she
took me by the hand and said her name was *Io* like the moon

and said *What sort of poems do you write, do you write them*
for pretty girls? I wondered what the hieroglyphs spelled, after all:

did those scared-looking buzzards and lilies and beetles
her father made deep in her heart spell out my name, tonight?

Once I was a picked flower, and my father made my head spin
by rubbing his palms together said Io, a Hawaiian girl, to me.

Song for a Play

The grief of little boys will make
them monsters, O,
but winter isn't here, hello.

The grief of little girls will make
them sad and sexy.
They'll dress themselves to be

undressed. They'll have an accident, no no.
The mad mothers, hello.
They all name cats after their long

dead brothers, but that isn't winter.
Winter has a long beard
and a hundred petty quarrels.

The suave fathers are leaving, O. They're leaving
but they wave. They wave
but let their watches stop. They like

the drama of the last tick as the spring
goes slack. Time
is their mausoleum.

The sad old men. When
the world forgets them
they read paperbacks and straighten up.

The ladies with the catheters and
bath benches are here
but winter, O, not winter, no.

But then the snow falls down
the yellow bus stops short
and skids, a tin accordion

there's one voyeur for every
widow's window
and it's winter, O, it's here, hello.

"The Glass Slipper"

In the blue light by the bathroom door, near the pay telephones, where
a weird staircase carpeted in red velour leads seemingly nowhere

a Scot is yelling *I'm A Scot* at a terrified dancer yelling back *I'm not*
and suddenly a bouncer carts him away, away; there I am standing

waiting for Mike to make his nightly rounds, astonishing Mike
with a dolphin for loneliness a dolphin for sadness a dolphin for fear

a hundred dolphins in harness drive his chariot and once a night
they appear before you and they're kind, they eat out of your hand.

In my dream I'm Audubon: with an ink for the belly of every bird.
I'm Audubon: with an ink for the injured bird I carry around inside.

In the blue light by the bathroom door, near the pay telephones, there
I wait for Mike to materialize, bold man, those smiling dolphins.

Self

Found not founded. Attacking only
from the back
like the Bengal tiger; afraid

of the face. Sweet-talking like the addict
coveting
another addict's stash. Fished from

my own trash like the feared
letter I heard later
held a birthday check.

Watched like the tiger from
a great height,
hollered out. Two-faced, masked

like the villager tricking
the tiger. Tricked
like the tiger. Founded on owned ground.

II

My Ravine

How will you know what my poem is like
    until you've gone down my ravine and seen

the box springs, mattresses, bookcases, and desks
    the neighboring women's college dumps each year,

somebody's hairdryer, someone's Herodotus
    a poem's dream landscape, one-half Latinate and

one-half shit, the neighboring women's college's shit?
    Wheelbarrow upon wheelbarrow a humpbacked

custodian hauls old dormitory furniture down
    and launches it watching it roll into the pile.

You won't know how my poem decides what's in,
    what's out, what decorum means and doesn't mean,

until you follow him home after work and see him
    going wild all night imagining those girls' old beds.

You won't know what I'm trying for until you hear
    how every fall in my backyard a swarm of deer

materializes, scavenging where the raspberries touched
  the radishes, now ploughed under, itching the lawn

for dandelions, stare at each other and wander
  bewildered down my ravine and turn into skeletons.

Poem

When I picture *1940* everyone poses
for me, as though I had the one

camera in the world. I cannot distract them
from their studied, ghoulish jolliness.

My grandmother is posing, yelling
Smile and my grandfather is horsing around

with a tire, making his biceps big. I
can't know the past, because the past

keeps arranging itself before my lens. People call
out *Here* and *Over here*, striking

their prewar, rural, easygoing stances.
That night, when I try again, everyone

is indoors, in parlors, reading quietly.
A woman rocking in and out of lamplight

studies me. The neighbor's
middle child died this afternoon.

Ward

I came quietly where
my grandmother
was an insect

in an iron hive.
No drop
of water fell

more quietly than I
fell through
the elevator shaft.

Then, on the ward,
I walked along
a hallway of formaldehyde

and glass.
A woman bent
herself in half

to scratch her coal-
black swollen foot.
Christ, one man's

forehead shone
white and dewy, like
a dolphin's belly.

Maiden never was who heard
the cribs fall
silent where her daughters were,

whose husband, frozen
still, berated her
one long year from

a piss-soaked chair.
What is awareness
here, so late, so close to night?

" . . . and yet the end must be as 'tis"

Soon, the laminated

tag, her name formed
in tangling lilies—

the t-shirts,
sweatshirts, robes

bought to replace
her old, coarse clothes,

the photographs this time
taken from the album, this time

held (crumbling, sciliate
with adhesive)

then the machine called

what: *Elysium*?
what: *halcyon*?

slumber, health, the old life,
memory—?

the truth
that underneath
her terry cloth

jersey is her body
unscarred, relieved

of her lost sons, as

she is helped into
a bath, her body

white, softening like an acorn

in a cup
of water—then "covered," clean

beneath
the kitsch
of death.

Visit

(Latin, "he saw," "he viewed")

Dying was not a change
of clothes, not a chance

to wear pajamas. I knew
his limbs were stiffening

for seven years, like one
of Dante's suicides kept

alive inside a tree. He knew
each ache would harden

him at last, he watched
it happen to himself, and

watched me watching him.
He saw me from his window

take a fly rod from
his shed and put it in my car.

He said "I saw you steal
my trout rod," which meant

"I haven't died." So I
returned it. Seeing him

die was like seeing a boy
inflate a sandwich bag

with breath, then empty it.
His flesh that had been

flesh, then Elm, was Ash.
I stayed a week, and

when he wasn't dying
anymore, I went away.

Anonymous Bust of a Man, c. A.D. 100 (Cyprus)

It is hard
to remember about the hardening man

he is alive, hard not
to hear

in the shrill nonsense

he speaks when he attempts to speak
the chirping

of a thrush, any
ordinary bird

hard to see
(but look) beneath

his sagging mask a face, once
flesh, now

lost, a planet—
barren and featureless as Pluto.

His eyes are not
two animals

playing tired, only
to pounce once

we pass by—he is no oak
to kiss beside.

His head twists on its stem.

Deer

My mother wishes
for a ghost's life.

She wants her dress to blow
against itself, not

against her skin, she asks
to be all breath, mind, gauze,

she hates the calcified *events*
composing her—

births, deaths, the old plateaus.

But when she begs
to lose all flesh she sees

her father's back bent
over a doe

he shot that morning, cleaning
her in our backyard.

He trims the bone of muscle,
gristle. Far off, he seems

to pray above her, or
to grieve, like Cephalus for his young wife;

but he is not grieving.

Evening, dinner, my grandmother
calling him inside. He takes

the hide intact into
his shed, hanging it to dry

like a woman's soaked gown.

One

The hour since midnight
was so full of me. The next hour will be better.

I will read Horace in
the quietest translation. I'll drink the water

in my water glass,
no more, no less.

The metaphors I'll use will be
those walking
humbly in the world already, foxes

without anything
to fear, the glow
of moonlight in their fur,

white grass before the other colors ripen.

Though she ransacked
my innocence,
transformed my house from silence

to the low gargle of sickness
and old age,
the night nurse with her pile of

crosswords on the cot, to her

the cot and crosswords,
night nurse
and formica table top were beautiful, almost a meadow.

I will do nothing more to night tonight.

III

Cicada

I

The "lily-like" cry from the tops
    of olive trees, or in my childhood

from maple trees that lined the road
    down to the beach: is it the call

of men held inside bodies so small
    they might have held them in their palms

once, when they were whole, who now
    are brittle and wail from treetops?

Forgetful of their bodies, these
    men housed themselves in music

when music like a new color
    declared itself on earth. Imagine

the silence before music, all
    the open mouths with no notes

coming out, like the mouths in paintings,
        underwater mouths, agape, the way

we picture suffering. It was
        like coming up for air when music

appeared here, and these men starved
        themselves for fear eating might stop

the beauty up. *Mousomania*,
        "music-madness"; and so the gods pitied

these men and pitying made them sing
        O *let me sing you past this night.*

II

And so the night I came home late
        and found one skating on my bedroom

mirror I was terrified, both for
        the poor soul trapped inside the green

contraption like a child fallen down
        a well, and for myself, forced to choose

whether to handle or to house
        the brittle man. I hate provoking

wildness in things—the strange dog's eyes
        met inadvertently, the housefly held

electric between panes; as a child
      I was so scared of my friends' fathers
I would hide when they got home from work.
      So all that night in bed I lay

awake, afraid at any moment the cicada
      might start crying as he did

perched on Eunomos's bow the time
      the fifth string broke, when

from an olive tree he dropped and
      landed where the slack string hung

and sang Eunomos's instrument
      "whole again and wholly beautiful."

III

Two people lie awake together
      in one bed. They do not speak.

Each knows the other is awake
      and knows the other knows.

Why can't they speak? As though
      a spell held them in place or some

god's architecture fastened
      their helpless limbs together—

as though their tongues were thick
                as loaves of bread inside their throats.

But this is love, each wants the other
                to escape the ceremonies of day,

each makes the night a little fantasy
                of night, a warm home decked with sleep.

Night after night they lie this way,
                no sleep, no speech, until one night

the telephone erupts and they sit up
                till dawn together, rocked by grief.

IV

The night I came home late and on
                my bedroom mirror saw that child

I imagined my own child: far
                from me because as yet unmade,

apart because imaginary, but the best
                boy there, the prettiest in that kingdom.

Baffled, he watches me as I assemble
                doctrine and dog shit, the junk

of adult life I learned watching TV.
                He gets to learn by watching me

pretend he's not alive, a lesson
        in resemblance and absence,

skill, refusal, all the usual lies
        you parse and press yourself against.

He gets to see me blank out slowly,
        the TV left on past the programming.

His mother will gradually grow to fear
        him there, in that vague place

since as he changes to my twin
        he changes to her enemy, the boy turned

to the man, the man uncannily
        like the father he could never know.

IV

Sometimes this song feels like a cure
        sometimes it makes the hurt much worse.

But it's the most brilliant defense—
        no judge ever lacked sympathy for this.

I'm making it up as I go along,
        but people like to think it's fate.

And so the night I came home late
        the actual cicada on my real mirror

scared me, for I hate handling anything
        I know needs my help fathoming

this maze of chairs and bottles and books,
        he mess I make of any room with my

unruly inwardness. Of course
        I couldn't kill it, where would I hide

the awful handful afterwards?
        That night I knew why old men lie

awake the night they start to die:
        the room is solemn, full of something

they can't scare away,
        their souls, or old childhood fears

they never solved, that stick to them
        like burrs or barnacles.

Their parents reappear at their bedside
        miming the ancient attitudes of

tenderness and rue, adoring them—
        and like the figures on a frieze

all those they loved appear as they were
        but mute, their eyes and lips sewn shut.

Then from inside the room a cry;
        and then the cicada flies away.

Stealing from Your Mother

I

Knowing her schedule you're half
way there. Watch the house dim and become

a museum; then

the familiar door, familiar
corridor, familiar
drawer. You know

the heirlooms from the junk.

You saw her cooing attachments form
over the years; now

you know where her best stuff is.

Her ring. Her wedding china.
The cameo of her grandmother.

Those are *pearls* that were
her pearls, and she

is somewhere else now, Florida
or on an errand; you know
several escapes.

There, in her closet, under
columns

of forgotten dresses, the sheer

dry-cleaner's plastic like a second skin—

Reward. Now it never wasn't yours.

II

The poem takes on a conscience. You wish
for your old self, unscrupulous,

pissed. You aren't exceptional.
Your wife wears pearls. Your real house

is a trick of light; the old one, gone,
is real enough to burn. Lacking

conviction, you will spend forever
sentencing yourself. You know

what you did. You know you know
what you did. No one is hearing your ornate confession.

Spade

I dreamed I was the spade
my mother used

to dig her marigolds in spring,
her *bloom* and *worry*.

Her digging, throwing, patting to bring
rows to life, each
bloom familiar

to worry, every row perfect, bloom,
rich dirt between, planned
absence and full, superfluous bloom—

I made the trench her hand proposed;

I was the pressure in her palm;

her *ache from planting*
was
my *presence in her life*.

Blueprint

I

I made God, God's
son, the angels and
the clouds of heaven

for my neighbor, an older boy
I loved and
whom I'd angered.

I made the clouds
from the unraveled
tips of cotton swabs.

Heaven was
a shoebox; building
heaven was fair

punishment
for calling him our pet name
within earshot

of his older friends.
Why do I see him, even
now: wild in shame, arms
waving, dangerous, trying
to erase
that syllable from air?

II

That year
he'd taken me
behind our shed to see

"what men and women do alone."
I was eight.
It was not his usual

locker-room patois.
He stacked
the twenty bleached-and-tattered

magazines atop
a quarter-cord of birch.
A light-blue plastic

tarp slapped
at the pile, keeping
the wood crisp

and combustible. Wax
pages, photographs:
the done-unto under

the doing, subduing
wave after
subduing wave:
girls sitting
still until
things settle.

Fact lost
in the shiny
satin drapery of fascination.

III

The Lord so loved the world
he sent
a steaming pile of

lasagna for
my ninth birthday.
A plate. Another. One

cascading square
waits on
a spatula; our priest

arrives. My mother greets him.
His peck
on my forehead

is full, unwelcome.
He squires me
from relative

to relative
collecting gifts:
sweater, eight-track, monster mask.

Father Tom in ordinary
clothes! I am
a special child.

Later, drunk, cursing
in Latin,
everyone in stitches,

he'll ash
his cigarette
on my bare arm.

IV

Another neighbor, later that same
summer. "Jamey":
contraband, a troublemaker, stammering

across the fence
at me *Who who
who who's your fa-*

father, fucker? Or
*Fucker doesn't
have a father.*

He'd read his Freud.
He knew
the blueprint of this poem, and others

I will have to write.
Then one
gray ordinary day
his father held him
down and nearly fucked
the life out of him.

Then he was quieter, and I
became sole
ruler of the neighborhood.

Purple Blouse

Then I dreamed I chose
the purple blouse my mother

wore the morning she conceived
me—dressed her, felt her

expectation as my own, her life
now distillate of her one wish

her saying *Yes* to the thing thrown
over her.

Matter

They found her purse in Africa.

*

Her watch was found, still
wound, in Maine; one

of her blouses was
discovered
floating in the Everglades, among

the yawning crocodiles.

The chilly metal eyeglasses I
still can feel
on my forehead, which I

would recognize beside
a hundred other pairs, were chosen from among

a hundred other pairs
by an ironic adolescent in Chicago—

*

matter can neither be created nor
destroyed: but where

is her firm voice outside
my bedroom door, where

is the slow comforting scrape and toss of snow
shoveling in 1981, the neighbor

showing off his blind
granddaughter, my 20/20 vision suddenly

obscene, embarrassing—

*

Tonight I find her bone
and pewter rosary

coiling on my bedside table.

A Salt Dish

Horace, Odes 2:16

At a table the size of my writing table, Horace's
happy man sits polishing his father's
salt dish, wearing the outer surface out, making it shine.

How small happiness seems, compared say
to the roller coaster they unveiled in
Florida, its corkscrew tail a football field long.

Today, I watched my friend descend his entryway
stairs in so much pain he seemed to move
through lava, lava pooling and pooling where

his limbs tried to take root, his light feet trying
to be heavy stone, not feather down, and
the fucked eventuality of his body worried every step.

Small meaningful trinkets for the rest of us. Heirlooms.
Something to hold a handful of material, some
vessel where the otherwise always-loosening self will settle.

The Afterlife of Objects

The lilac behind glass, the old hoe brought inside.

> *I dreamed I lay asleep wrapped*
> *in the lilac's stifling embrace.*

> *I woke and found the old hoe in my bed,*
> *my limbs were caked with loam.*

The crumbling mica of old dust jackets.

> *I dreamed I was covered with the chalk*
> *of flaking pages of military histories.*

> *I woke and found I'd authored*
> *Vermont's evacuation plans.*

The cellar where canned meat was stored.

> *In my dream, the Kennedys invite*
> *me to a picnic, they are just like us.*

> *My grandfather wrote the code*
> *that kept the Cold War hanging there.*

The old hoe brought inside. The fly rod I tried to steal.

I thought his eyes were tired
because his arms and legs were tied.

I never wished him dead,
I wished him blind.

IV

Peach Tree

When did I plant this peach tree in my sleep and why
now does it seem to bloom
as though in answer to a prayer?

I did not ask to see the tree extend its bough so far
it almost disappeared
but finally unfolded this white flower.

I lived so long fearing the world's quaint
insufficiencies were mine—
as air would conjure earth, earth, air

I stared at the little life made in my name, and thanked
the immediate and thanked the near.
I thanked my mother and my father and my other

mother and my other father, but when I
thanked them all I still
had fearfulness inside of me, mysterious.

As water conjures fire and fire, water, I discovered
that within I bore a boy who bore
my own name whom I had not thanked.

That night I dreamed of the field
of folk—the man with the fistful
of radishes, the passionate one, and the neighbor

whose granddaughter's eyes were closing for ever
and ever, and the hippie babysitter
with the white dog on the white leash, and

the CPA with the lemon Bonaventure. All seemed
to look on me with pity, as though
they knew my fate, knew its necessity.

I woke and there on the brilliant field outside
my window they were gathered,
a congregation circling the boy

I bore who bore my name, all staring
at the little flower on
the peach tree I had planted in my sleep.

Coda

to a friend

That convex mirror was a gift your drunkenness gave you, pried
from your elevator door one night. Elevators and small, elevator-like

restaurants, and the driver's seats of rented cars are where I picture
you. You take after your ancestors, butchers and last-makers, shaping

the slaughter behind culture, warp of laughter, woof of sadness.
You are an elegist at heart, but loss shocks you; your drawers are piled

with cuff links and tie clips somebody's uncle's uncle wore. The watch
you wear keeps ticking away, away, from the watch-shop where, deep

inside the last century, it caught your grandfather's eye. Even then it ticked
toward your wrist, toward this restaurant nearing closing time: the wine,

the underdone lamb. On 13th Street the present just got out; back home
the past (part theft, part gift) reflects close up how far away you seem.

After Ovid

It is sure misfortune
for a child to marry.

God's will is otherwise, and so
the child I called

sweet names died while still
indistinct to me. Picturing

her now is like picturing
the moon close up, the chalky surface of the moon.

The next was blameless—pretty,
more or less, but not a prize.

Once I surprised her kneading dough
for that night's supper and

she shuddered afterward
for hours. Now

my love, my third, best wife
sobs constantly for me.

She counts my exile on
a calendar. Why must I picture

her betraying me?

    Dawn, an all night party, and she
    is lying on a banquet table strewn

    with half-eaten plums, gorged bread,
    upended drinking cups, wine running

    from the table in a narrow ribbon, hair
    back, begging for the cocks of twenty

    drunkards lining up for her

Thank God my mother died before
she saw
her boy brought here by boat, dropped

here beside the Danube.

Mechanical Wall, 1982

on my birthday

In school a wall kept the other half
        of the sixth-grade class mysterious
to us. Miss Rush would make it part
        on holidays, for awful parties where

we weren't allowed to flirt. When her echo,
        Miss Costello, shouted *Go* the wall slowly
withdrew into itself and we were face
        to face with kids who seemed that instant

artificial, blown from molten glass or molded
        in papier-mâché —not kids we knew already
anyway, from recess or from last year's class.
        It should have felt like we were staring

at ourselves, because we were; in one
        case, James Guillette beheld his twin
brother Marcel slowly revealed by
        the parting wall, and all of us knew the insides

of each other's houses, the divorces, mothers
          who sucked from bottles, sisters who got cancer or
who moved away to live in the trailers
          of older men who treated them like daughters.

We knew each other's lives by heart. Maybe
          that's why we looked so hard at one another
or why I peer at my own face today (same
          face as yesterday) in the mirror as

aghast sometimes I peer out our back window
          at unseasonable weather, snow in April, tight buds
this February on the cherry. Miss Rush
          was thirty, childlike, and unattractive.

She had once been a nun but now
          lived with a woman on the edge of town. We tried
to hurt her as best we could about it, but
          somehow she stayed nice. That pissed us off.

Dream of the End of Reading

First my books grew stiff
brass clasps like the books monks read.

A hush enshrouded them. They were
as stern and foreign as a cooling meteorite.

Then a steady rain fell every day
for weeks, soaking them through

a window I left open, rusting
them shut. Nothing would pop

them free. I thought they'd grow
mysterious as stars, inspiring speculation;

or by their unforthcoming purity
and order I might prophecy

my own behavior. But they were
as they were, mere

objects in a world of objects. I thought
I'd miss the page: arena

of my lifelong melodrama, dressing
each morning for a date

with truth, then restless
all day, glued to the clock

and telephone and mail, disheveled,
mad, stood up; then drunk

or stoned all night to dull
the loneliness of nothing

happening, no insight
more or less than vapor, no handle

not already dull from
habitual use. I never read one through.

Leverett Circle

What helping him involved was first
       his helping me. What helping me

required was his cradling my sandwich
       in his lap, jeans black with rainwater.

My sandwich was his freight
       and he was mine, and O the sharp

curb scared us both, two strangers, as
       of course the rain rains equally upon

the deli and the hospital. And when
       I handed him my sandwich he

said *thank you* as though I'd given it
       away, and later when he gave

it back I thanked him as I'd thanked
       the woman working at the deli

earlier. The world is full
       of curbs. The world is full of ruts

that take a wheel wherever they will
       and furrows any wheel will follow

and so I asked him too soon *You*
    got it from here, Sir? and he had

to answer *No, please get me over*
    there: there, some sort of border

under my awareness, some mark
    on the blank brick walk. When he returned

my sandwich carefully it didn't mean
    I'd earned it back, but that I could

begin not knowing him again; and when
    he thanked me far from *I am new* it meant

I'll wheel myself from here.

Self-Storage

Bring me your amateurish try
at taxidermy, fleur-de-lys

upholstered chair, flea-bitten oven mitt, replica Mars lander, old suit, bad

choice, wrong turn.
Bring me your freak, your odd, your ugly

rug, dull knife, dull life. Threatening noise heard
over and over in your skull, a bell

how many thousand decibels
loud, how much distraction, sadness, everything

is safe with me and out of sight.

*

America the widow
sorting through his drawer

of fisted socks. The ice shedding
itself inside the water glass.

The diagnosis. The dozen
childlike men begging for medication.

The monkey screaming behind
iron bars. Tender objects:

the dried corsage. America
a certain model

motorcycle, rare Beatles
butchered baby cover

safe, all safe,
all out of sight.

*

Are you the phone call
or the military

base, *North Carolina*
or *Vermont*, the rapist or my
aunt sent

far away for basic training,
senator
or sergeant, mother's tears

or father's stern
embarrassed
order to shut up? The den

or the phone, the voice
or the street noise, or television's

usual banal exuberance? America
they wanted

her to marry him.

*

Of all things seen
beside the highway I

am most like you. The stories
of lunatics and pack rats

storing old newspapers
broken bottles

scribbles animal remains
are true. Also

the corpses. Also
the stolen stereo.

A priest stores
jeweled chalices in me, no questions asked.

*

O pension everyone
agreed upon.

O slave, sieve, place
to put the precious useless things.

Aubade

I want to build but not
what I prayed
to build all the shrinking May nights, the lengthening

November nights, I want to build instead a bird's
body entirely
out of carpenter's right angles

and joinery, vices and saws, a lifelike bird!
I've made my own life
neat as a knot, tight as a fist—

strange how easily the ordinary becomes
ordinary, you and I
and the little vinyl modules we look back on

with regret or tenderness, and then
the strings and horns
and then the whole orchestra piles it on!

There's a nugget of what I want
to be in the statement
I am lonely most of the time, and tired of love.

It explains why I always get caught
in the bathroom making
my face make cruel expressions back at me.

But if I build for us a little bird
of pine and nails, we'll
hold the homemade, fidgety body in our hands

all dawn and, since we made it and
can prove it, even
its terror, even its fearful call, we'll call it ours.

Orange Tree

Dream of the bitter
greenish flesh of a tiny orange tree we grew

upstairs in our
bow window: I am eight or nine.

In life, I hoped
the flesh
would end up sweet

the way the fist-sized oranges in grocery bags turn

sweet, the way bought fruit does
almost always. But in my dream

I asked a man, my grandfather
but with the face
of an actor, playing him better

than he played himself, an actor

playing me
convincingly, a phony rented orange tree so real, the whole

set crafted by a new technique to look
just as I left it—
I asked

*

*Sir, will you
cook these oranges?*

Yes said the man, my grandfather, and led
me to an oven
where the green flesh of the orange tree turned orange

for me, sweet and edible, whatever

I could want.

*

I woke and spoke these words to you, since you
were nearest; and
you heard, since you were there.

NOTES

"The Sensible Present Has Duration": The title is taken from William James's *The Principles of Psychology*.

"Self": Woodcutters in the Ganges delta wear wooden masks on the back of their heads to confuse Bengal tigers, who only attack from the back. The poem is indebted to Elisa New's *The Line's Eye: Poetic Experience, American Sight*.

"Boston": The phrase in quotes is from Henry James's *The American Scene*.

"Cicada": The Greek adjective describing the cicada's song, *leirios*, is often translated "lily-like." The poem's source is the myth of the cicadas in Plato's *Phaedrus*.

"After Ovid": The poem is indebted to passages in Ovid's *Tristia*, book IV.